HAJI AS PUPPET:

AN ORIENTALIST BURLESQUE

Other books by Roger Sedarat:

Dear Regime: Letters to the Islamic Republic
Ghazal Games
Foot Faults: Tennis Poems

HAJI AS PUPPET:

AN ORIENTALIST BURLESQUE

poems

Roger Sedarat

For Sahar —
It's an honor to share
this collection with you!

WINNER OF THE 2016 TENTH GATE PRIZE

Series Editor, Leslie McGrath
THE WORD WORKS
Washington, D.C.

ACKNOWLEDGMENTS

Thank you to the journals that first published these poems:

> *Two Review*: "Haji As Prophet."
> *The J Journal: New Writing on Justice*: "Haji As Post-Colonizer."
> *The Other Voices International Project*: "The Prophet As Analysand,"
> "The Prophet As Sufi Tour Guide of the Old Country," and
> "Haji As Directionless Prophet."
> *Cerise Press: A Journal of Literature, Arts, and Culture*: "Haji As
> Prophet Defends his (T)rutful (t)one."

"This Little Haji" and "Haji's Rubaiyyat" first appeared in *Dear Regime: Letters to the Islamic Republic* (Ohio University Press).

And thank you to venues where Haji poems have been performed:

> Summer Institute for Social Justice and Applied Poetics. Bowery
> Poetry Club, New York City, 2010: "Revolution."
>
> Geraldine R. Dodge Poetry Festival, Waterloo Village, Stanhope,
> 2008: "Haji Hic Ups in the Middle East."
>
> Poetry Salaam/The Fatoosh Ensemble Present: "We Are Gaza."
>
> Montclair State University, 2009: "Haji Hic Ups in the Middle East."
>
> Literature of Resistance: An Afternoon of Solidarity with the
> Iranian People. Bowery Poetry Club, New York City, 2009:
> "Revolution from the Outside In."

Performances of Haji poems available online at YouTube:

> "The Spin," "Haji As Appropriator of the Islamic Revolution,"
> "Haji's Blue Guitar" (excerpt), "Haji As Puppet."

CONTENTS

11 Cast
13 Advertisement
14 Advertisement
15 Precursor to Haji's Curtain Call
17 Haji As Puppet
24 The Puppet As Analysand
26 Haji As Directionless Puppet
28 Haji's Blue Guitar
31 Haji as Post-Colonizer
34 Haji Hic Ups in the 21st Century
36 Faux Revolution, 2007
39 When the mullah fell asleep...
40 When the puppet made his way west...
42 Haji As Beer Boy
49 Prelude to a Postmodern Persian Puppet Dance
50 Iran As Spectacle (an Orientalist Burlesque)
58 Haji's Campaign to Support the Troops Becomes a Real Drag
60 Haji's Recipe for a Televised Disaster
61 Haji's Scarlet Letter
62 This Little Haji
63 Haji Defends His (T)ruthful (T)one
64 Haji As Appropriator of the Islamic Republic
69 When like Frankenstein's monster they install human eyes
        into the head of the Persian poet puppet...
70 Elemental Translation: Water
72 Haji's Ekphrastic Mental Mapping
74 Haji vs. Rostam
76 Haji Haiku
77 Po Biz
78 Haji's Waterboarding
80 Lunar Politics
81 Haji's Rubaiyyat

83   Ah Gee, Haji

86   Return to the Circus Animals

89   About the Author / About the Artist

90   Other Word Works Books

We are but puppets; heaven but the puppet player.

—Omar Khayyam

Well, I got the fever down in my pockets.
The Persian drunkard, he follows me.

—Bob Dylan

CAST

Haji . . . . Childhood nickname given by poet's Iranian family.

Haji . . . . First name of pseudonym (Haji Khavari) used to protect identity of postmodern Persian writer living in Iran whose work poet translates.

Haji . . . . Muslim male successfully completing the pilgrimage (Hajj) to Mecca.

Haji . . . . A derogatory term for Middle Easterners used by racist westerners, often those in the U.S. military, comparable to "gook" during the Vietnam war.

Haji . . . . Protagonist of 19th century picaresque novel, *The Adventures of Hajji Baba of Ispahan*, by British author J.J. Morier. This best-selling Orientalist satire, written as if biographically reported by a native, reinforced a belief in the civilizing superiority of the west. Morier developed his caricature out of his friendship with the first Persian ambassador to London. Upon publication of the novel, the Iranian diplomat wrote to the author: "That very bad book, sir. All lies sir."

Haji . . . . Protagonist of same 19th century novel rendered into Persian by translator M.H. Isfahani, who re-appropriated earlier Orientalist stereotypes as he changed the text into his native language.

Haji . . . . Star (played by garden variety non-Middle Eastern/vanilla flavor of the month actor John Derek) of 1954 American movie, *The Adventures of Hajji Baba*, based on the book by Morier.

Haji . . . . Subject of song "Hajji Baba (Persian Lament)" sung by legendary crooner Nat King Cole featured in American movie based on the book by Morier.

PRECURSOR TO HAJI'S CURTAIN CALL

A mock-Persian carpet, made to look ancient and well-trodden-upon by generations, hangs as curtain before the audience. The restless spectators take the tapestry for granted. Anxious to get on with the show, they blindly chant for Haji (*Haji! Haji! Haji! Haji! Haji!*).

But one nameless Iranian-American boy, seemingly without parents, silently plays "I spy with his little hybrid eye." As if pre-programmed by the program, he sees a mosaic of Haji's trickster persona woven tightly into the tapestry:

+ Walt Whitman sewed beside Hafez, Haji's needlework forcing their eternally long bearded kiss.

+ Standing as one of the U.S. hostages in faded 1979 photograph, Haji lifts his blindfold to wink at the camera.

+ Haji, beside handcuffed Mohammad Mosaddegh post-CIA coup, slyly reaching for the guard's keys.

+ Dipping his finger in the Bush/Cheney recipe for Niger uranium used to justify the invasion of Iraq and subsequent destabilization/neo-colonization of the nation, Haji literally licks the yellowcake batter to shock and awe a media feeding frenzy.

+ Within the meta-portrait of boys weaving this carpet, Haji sticks his limbs into the loom, disrupting the ancient machinery of his own cultural production.

Despite his best rehearsed intentions, when Haji surfaces at show time to teach the audience a lesson, he finds his part rewritten.

HAJI AS PUPPET

"A poem is an event, not a record of an event."
—Robert Lowell

1.
Prefabricated Haji stood against his will
affixed to invisible strings
under an imaginary puppeteer,
forcing his audience to consider
the idea of creativity
controlled by the divine.
A pre-recorded poem
played on miniature speakers
beside the make-shift ladder.

Made to follow pre-written lines
tied to his loose limbs,
a Disneyland child captain
whose little boat follows
the pre-charted course
on a rail in 2 feet of water,
Haji stood in America
as insignificant as
"Comedian as Letter C,"
insofar as Wallace Stevens
subjected poor Crispin
to his fated aesthetic,
rusty lines from romantic times
pre-ordaining a journey
to nowhere.

2.
How Haji tried opting out
of the system,
knifing taught strings
that schooled all movements
of his being.

The MOST HIGH simply yanked him
back into place.

How he resented assumptions
of himself as entertainment.
Haji hated monkey dances.
Unlike others of his generation,
stood ashamed of a writer identity.
How ridiculous, the parade of self
at conferences like AWP, careerism
of dribble and drabble,
superficial *belle-lettrists*
praise of hollow words,
devoid of the divine.

Like Sylvester the Cat's son—
Junior suffering succotash
seeing his father
beat up by the mouse
who knows the audience
is just a baby kangaroo—
given his right
to assert himself in public,
Haji would live

with a paper bag over his head,
sighing "Oh Father!"
like the shamed kitten
and call it a day.

Shame for the latest one-hit neo-surrealist wonders
who write about aspirin sprouting from tomato plants.

Shame for the MFA's and PhD's in creative writing.
Shame for the cartoon promotions
of the latest published collections.

3.
But the puppeteer above
forced him to throw away
his bag of antithetical trickery.
This GREAT CREATOR would settle for nothing less
than human decadence,
the poet as greatest-
worst example of a poem.

Made to make a literal
ass out of himself
on all fours,
kicking and hee-hawing
through the poem,
the more he struggled against the idea
of his body as spectacle,
the sillier he appeared.

Looking up, Haji could almost hear
the ALPHA and OMEGA
appropriate his verse,
asking him as failed performer,

"Little Ham, who made thee?
Dost thou know who made thee,
Gave thee life and bid thee feed
By the stream and oe'r the mead."

4.
Having right-sized his subject,
the puppeteer yanked him up
by his boot strings, a rabid Republican
controlling a democratic sheep,
dime a dozen in the world of poetry
who invariably just put folks to sleep.

Considering the tension of exile
from his native Iran
the ULTIMATE BIOGRAPHER
wrote his ending
as political elegy.

In light of Haji's pathetic dreams
of leading a rock n' roll revolution,
he found himself made to reference
U2's "Sunday Bloody Sunday"
with accompanying images
of an age-old crackdown
on the streets of Tehran
screened at Met-Life Stadium
in New Jersey.

Compelled to wear Bono's sunglasses,
the FORCE beyond his control
told him to introduce
the recollected moment in absurdity
by leading the audience with a cheer.

5.
"No!" said Haji. "I'm sick of having
to face this western music!

I want to read my own poems
from the page!"

The puppeteer just shook his invisible head,
commanding the monkey dance instead.

"I," said Haji, motioning the audience to scream "I!"
"R," continued the poet-toy soldier.
"A," yelled the punk, in formal anarchy.
"N," concluded the rebellious conformist.

"Iran! Iran! Iran! Ra, Ra, Iran!"

(Cue U2's "Sunday Bloody Sunday" drum intro,
played loud enough to shake the stage.)

Add to this the influence of a *taziyeh*,
Shia-Islam passion play for Hussein,
rightful heir of Mohammad's rule
martyred on the streets of Karbala.

How heavy the metal of Haji's belt
as he beat his back in time,
paybacks for crimes
as mock-martyr,
appropriator
of a botched
revolution.

Sure, Bono did it too,
but he's Bono,
not insignificant Haji
who'd simply make bad mimicry
of an ageless rock star
in purple sunglasses.

6.
The noose awaits,
ultimate string for this puppet.

(Noose drops from ceiling.)

Why even put up a fight,
making further spectacle
of his insignificance?

7.
When asked to choose a last meal,
he requests stale bread and water,
anti-communion
for a passive audience,
symbol for death
and molding afterlife,
of banal attempts
at artifice.

And picking up a piece of the hard bread
Haji breaks it in two, saying,

"This is my body caught
in the condition of literature
in the 21st century;

take what's left of it
and feed it
to the New York pigeons."

And picking up the cup of lukewarm tap water
he continued, saying,

"This is my blood,
empty of real significance,
use it as ink to write an epitaph
on the sidewalk."

8.
When asked for any last words,
despite trying to summon
the verse of Hallaj,
authentic Muslim martyr,
he heard himself reciting
one of the million
best American poems
written without conviction
against his will,
then felt his head pulled
through the noose.

9.
So ends Haji as hangman.
Stretched to his limits, he's made to bow
before a universe he'd never choose
to create.

10.
(Cue Ziggy Stardust.)

THE PUPPET AS ANALYSAND

And the New York psychoanalyst said to Haji,
"Speak uncensored of yourself."

And Haji replied:
"Simple Simon met a pie man."

And the analyst said, "You're resisting."

And Haji slouched his shoulders and folded his arms,
displaying the universal body language
of hostility.

And the analyst said, "Think of it like
the rough draft of a poem, Haji;
let your words escape without editing."

And Haji the poet-puppet ventriloquized,
"Huffy Haji...hid the day!"

"That's John Berryman, Haji!" exclaimed the analyst.
"Why do you feel compelled to copy
when invited to speak for yourself?"

"Because," replied Haji, "you're only as sick as your secrets."

"Berryman said that too!" exclaimed the analyst.

"All the more reason to rein myself in," replied Haji.

"So you want to stay sick?" asked the psychoanalyst.

"No," replied Haji. "I want to stay original
in this age of the memoir, originally coopting
a self-defining tradition."

"Is that where Iran comes in?" asked the analyst.
"Can you speak to us (i.e. the 'U.S.') of Iran?"

"A certain psychoanalyst," explained Haji,
"administered a Rorschach test to a certain
analysand, the usual black splatter
requiring interpretation.

'Within a black butterfly,'
said the analysand,
'I see oil from Iran
giving rise
to western fantasies

of nuclear fallout,
projections of a holocaust
hanging dark clouds
over the region.'

I haven't…I mean…the analysand
hasn't been sleeping so well at night;
even with earplugs and blinders,
evil scenarios haunt his dreams."

HAJI AS DIRECTIONLESS PUPPET

And the black butterfly repeatedly crashed
into his own reflection,
first a flutter then a thud,
a thudder of meaning,
miniature *méconnaissance*,
quixotic wing beats,
appearance of the void,
impenetrable black hole,
spectral spider web,
insect signifier
writing and erasing
the know-nothing poem;
"ink-a-dink a bottle of ink";
surreptitious selection
a-natural, closeted desire
to see the desire of
the other;
reductive darkness
labeled "midnight black"
rendering "the difficult
a little hard to see";
rhetoric of academia,
turgid circumlocution,
dead letters subsuming the spirit,
the world of forms
flatlining on the hospital monitor,
inconsequential mourning,
eclipsed cosmology
turning and turning...

"The butterfly *c'est moi*"
dit the Flaubert wannabe,
Etch-A-Sketch shaker,
eye-mask somnambulist
stumbling through the eternity
of a summer night.

HAJI'S BLUE GUITAR

Unlike so many mischief-makers,
Haji's the antithesis of trickster,
flavorless factoid, mimicry of mundane.
Having read, with great indifferent interest
Marjorie Perloff's *Unoriginal Genius*
and Kenneth Goldsmith's *Uncreative Writing*
he allays all anxiety of influence,
surrendering to the lines of Stevens' poetry
on seemingly pre-programmed strings
of his own blue guitar,
travis-picking the master's first three sections
as he circulates copies of Picasso's famous painting
to remind the audience
how the original old guitarist
played against a background of blue
expression of the artist's grief,
x-rays revealing three figures
behind the visible oil paint,
ghostly bones of a close friend's suicide.
But those were different times.
Even Stevens' blue inversion
declaring the guitar a thing unto itself
ultimately changed things
upon the blue guitar.
Not so with Haji,
for whom things as they are
remain just as they are.
Thus he attempts to replicate
this reductive spirit of self,
received reality in the 21st century,
rewriting Pound's modernist maxim,
"Make it new" underpinning most verse

with an admonition of the tradition
inherited in his own time:
Let it be real.

Years ago at a hole-in-the-wall falafel café near Columbia University, Edward Said tapped Haji on the shoulder, asking him to pass the hot sauce. So began a heated interchange between postcolonial theorist and postmodern practitioner.

HAJI AS POST-COLONIZER

And a hybrid identity asks Haji,
"Speak to us of power."

And Haji replies,
"Intersecting circles of oppressor and oppressed
create a new voice transcending origins.
The wind owns the machine of production,
manufacturing cultural material
through agency
of Emerson's colonizing consciousness,
transparent self-revelation:

'I am nothing / I see all.'

Between intersecting eyeball as first circle
and perceived landscape as close second,
formative free play
of Shakespeare's *The Tempest*
staged in the rediscovered Middle-
East,
Taliban as Caliban
fighting powers that be,
meaning American Prospero
wrapped in a hegemonic blanket
of stars and stripes,
achieves symbolic victory,
the CIA agent puppeteering
the burqaed questioner
who became fluent in Dari
while taking long walks
on the Harvard campus,
linguistic double agent
code switching on command,

his bilingual source book
casting denotative spells
upon such primitive objects
in the old country
as sticks and stones.

Truth, says Nietzsche, is hard.
'And what we have here,'
says the ruthless old fucker
in *Cool Hand Luke*,
'is failure to communicate.'

Allow me (says Haji) to give a jeremiad
so despairing, you'd just as well
shatter the mirror like Charlie Sheen
in *Apocalypse Now*,
or join Kurtz at the end
of *The Heart of Darkness*,
'The horror, the horror!'"

The hardest thing about humanity
is that it's essentially inhuman.
Of course Haji too joins in the necessary correctives,
calling for justice,
but undermining the freedom fight's
the problem of imposing, "Do unto others"
to Freud in Austria
when the Nazis are coming.

Of course it's more complicated,
the age old question of free-agency,
and of course Haji's for the good guys,
likes to count himself among them,
but don't we all?

Say what you will about oppressor and oppressed,
the tension drives the story,
forms the lyric power, etc.
Otherwise, we're struck
with Shirley MacLaine's
namby-pamby
netherworld verse.

But what of transcendent Rumi,
the mystics who confronted power
(even faux seers like Emerson)
at the point of language itself?

Haji too wishes it were all
a mere war of words with the divine,
longs to feel a true connection

to the ultimate colonizer
that creates
and divides
all creation
(see *Genesis*).

HAJI HIC UPS IN THE 21ST CENTURY

Too much falafel or philosophy? (*hic up*)
Before we make him eat peanut butter (*hic up*)
or sneak behind him to pop a paper bag, (*hic up*)
let's hear how too much reasoning (*hic up*)
bubbled up in his stomach, (*hic up*)
how like a needle scratch on an old LP (*hic up*)
the world kept turning while remaining stuck (*hic up*)
in the Middle East, Mid-(*hic up*)
dle East. Yes, he's tried drinking a glass of milk (*hic up*)

upside down; it didn't work. (*hic up*)
Too much absurd laughter as talking heads reiterate the stories (*hic up*)
and televise decapitations. (*hic up*)

Haji leaked a little laugh, little laugh, (*hic up*)
little laugh, Haji leaked a little laugh (*hic up*)
but why he didn't know. CNN imposed itself, (*hic up*)
a corporate construct upon the world, (*hic up*)
every airport blaring the same sights and sounds, (*hic up*)
every hotel room featuring explanations in the Mid-(*hic up*)
dle East. Images of teenagers in Gaza on the western news (*hic up*)
got Haji so stoned, he scaled the walls of reason, (*hic up*)
pulled down his pants with uproarious laughter (*hic up*)
to start a revolution of one, (*hic up*)
breaking out in song like a Persian alley cat: (*hic up*)

I got the cleanest meanest penis. (*hic up*)
You've never seen this stroke of genius. (*hic up*)

Only Notorious BIG could capture the moment in lyrics. (*hic up*)
Or else Haji imbibed forbidden booze (*hic up*)
when nobody was looking, (*hic up*)
sneaking behind the mosque at midnight (*hic up*)

with a bottle marked XXX, (*hic up*)
talking to *jinn* on his cell phone, nursing hangovers (*hic up*)
behind newspapers in his neighborhood coffee shop. (*hic up*)

To hang up the hic up one needs God more than ever, (*hic up*)
a transcendent breath of fresh air from the top of Mt. Ararat (*hic up*)
or from the shore of the Caspian Sea. (*hic up*)
Haji must return to nature (*hic up*)
with a copy of Rumi's *Collected Works* in one hand (*hic up*)
and Thoreau's *Walden* in the other, (*hic up*)
an ignorant hick receiving his comeup-(*hic up*)
pance.

FAUX REVOLUTION, 2007

And a protester on the streets of Tehran tweeted,

"How do we know if this revolution's real? #Haji'spoliticalpunditry"

And Haji replied:

"A certain cat failed to get
a certain freedom fighter's tongue,
leaving him speaking for a nation
he feared could cut off his head.
Let it be known on Facebook
he'd teach the Grand Ayatollah a lesson
despite his irrational terror
of Basiji goons
kicking down his door
in suburban America,
dragging him out
into a starless night
as he screams,
'I told you'd they'd come!'
to his incredulous family.
You think he'd learned his lesson 30 years ago
with Khomeini-men who discovered
his Savaki uncle in hiding
marching the colonel
to a firing squad.

Before the poetry reading in support of protestors,
he rouses himself at 0500,
repeatedly dunks his head
into a sink of cold water
and writes a too self-conscious poem

under pressure of forced confession,
re-inscribing guilt of doing nothing
but appropriating real events into verse.
Dressed in black,
he puts on his son's toy police helmet,
(aware of the irony that the visor's
tinted Mousavi green),
and pokes himself out the door
with an umbrella figuratively charged
like an electric prod
onto the subway
and into NYC's Bowery Poetry Club.

On cue he starts a poem
in the voice of a persona named Haji
about speaking up to get
beaten down,
during which he smacks his back,
Shia'-martyr style for Hussein,
visions of Neda—
post-modern icon of the prelude
to a revolution—
sending strike upon strike
through his brain.

A poet caught in the performance of his life.
You think it's so easy standing up for yourself
when the repressive regime you're fighting
has less blood on its hands than a land proclaiming
idyllic freedom? Sure, he cried this 4th of July
as the band played 'God Bless America.'
Later, at relative peace with hypocrisy,
as suburbanites slept in their beds,

he climbed out of his attic window
and onto his roof, shouting,
'Death to the dictator!' and 'God is great'
as random fireworks rained overhead.
Dogs howled. Rows of houselights came on.
Folks emerged on their lawns in their PJ's.
Finally, a heavy-set neighbor
in wife-beater and boxers yelled,

'Hey buddy, you're in Jersey! It's a free country.
Now shut the fuck up and let us get some sleep!'

Here stands Haji, silenced on the stage.
Nobody even takes his picture,
the consequence
of being
in the wrong place
at the right time."

WHEN THE MULLAH FELL ASLEEP...

his marionette untied his own strings.
Feeling affined to those still controlled
by Muslim Muppeteers,
he swiped a can
of his savage set designer's
dark spray paint
to calligraphy this story
on the concrete wall:

A political dissident
in Tehran's notorious Evin Prison
sitting in a solitary cell
without ink to write
another revolutionary poem
began going crazy without stimulus.

After hours of countless prayers,
his forehead scarred by the floor,
a black butterfly flitted through the bars
and into his open hand,
the blood of Imam Hussein oozing
through a clenched fist.

WHEN THE PUPPET
MADE HIS WAY WEST...

he got caught by Israeli soldiers,
hung up in mockery
on the Great Wall of Gaza
beside Banksy's balloon girl.
Despite taunts
from children
on both sides
of politics
he insisted
on his sermon:

"In 1987, when defense minister Yitzhak Rabin in Israel
ordered soldiers to break the bones
of protesters waving the Palestinian flag,
Haji longed to walk the streets
holding two halves of a watermelon,
ubiquitous signifier of displaced country,
green skin, red fruit, black seeds, and white rind
reproducing the real thing.

But when Haji samuri-sworded his melon,
a white dove flew into the streets of Gaza,
its neck bleeding from an inadvertent cut.
After flying through smoke from burning tires,
it crashed into the image of an olive branch covered
with graffiti on a billboard."

Haji's black face, painted with used motor oil, reflects western images of the Middle East. When he arrives turbaned on a camel with a cartoon saber, he's not so much trying to subvert the gaze of network news as reiterate the status quo. (It's a dirty job, but somebody's got to do it.)

HAJI AS BEER BOY

Having tied up the ancient saki,
mystic wine boy of the royal court
who insured Hafez
stayed drunk with desire,
Haji shaved his beard,
jammed his knees
into a pair of kids Nikes
and waddled into an audition,
heeding his casting call:

Child-actor needed
in cute commercial
for King of Beers.

> *

TAKE ONE

Bearded baby
child as Father
of the man
cracks open
a Tall Boy.
"American Strong!"
grunts Haji
into the camera,
flexing his bicep
(cue burp),
his distinctive belch,
putrid potpourri
spewing
pancake make-up
& genetically modified yeast,

the aura of his stardust
passing
the screen test.

     *

TAKE TWO

His best George Bush
post Hurricane Katrina
to FEMA director
Michael Brown:
"Heh heh heh
heck of a job,
America!"

(Winks at camera,
belch as emerging
catch phrase.)

     *

TAKE THREE

On all fours,
one eye ringed
with charcoal,
Walkman headphones
around his neck
like a collar,
reprising the role
of Super Party Animal
Spuds MacKenzie.

(Burrrrrp™!!!)

*

TAKE FOUR

New take
on ancient
Persian
pederasty:
toes painted,
legs shaven
for short-shorts,
nubile
beer girl
in place
of wine boy.

*

TAKE FIVE

(Cue deep upbeat didactic voice of male narrator:)

"As a toddler
he dug in the sandbox
& struck oil"

(footage of child Haji
as Saudi sheik).

"He took lunch money
from the bullies
and started a hedge fund"

(footage of child Haji
having milk & cookies
on his own jet).

"He makes his teachers
stay after school"

(footage of child Haji
making women laugh
in teachers' lounge).

(Cue child Haji
speaking to camera:)

"I don't always drink beer,
but when I do,
please don't tell my Mom!"

(Takes a swig,
loud burp™!!!!!!)

      *

TAKE SIX

Haji in rhinestone chaps
& pink boots
surrounded by gay cowboys,
musky oil riggers
in wife-beaters,
Navy men closet-clubbing
New York Fleet Week,
bare-chested fireman
who just climbed out
of a Playgirl calendar.

(Cue narrator:)

"Macho men
drink mucho
light beer."

As Haji's cast
of all-star studs
lifts him up
on their broad shoulders
Haji cracks open
a Tall Boy,
toasts the camera
in his new role
as King of Queens.

*

(Out)take Seven

Collective chug-a-lug
of Tall Boys
with camera still rolling
& Haji on broad shoulders
of his village people.

(Cue Haji:)

"Okay, guys, all together
on three: 1, 2, 3!"

BURRRRRRRRP™!!!

*

TAKE EIGHT

Tiny tot Haji
sits atop
two phonebooks
to reach
the steering wheel,
designated driver
of drunk white clowns,
gringos and gringas
salsa dancing
out of rhythm,
soulless celebration
in a Ford Fiesta,
Haji's horn honking
La Cucaracha!
announcing his arrival
as king of the cracker
carnival.

(Cue concerned male voice reminding drivers to party
responsibly.)

*

TAKE NINE

Enter American soldiers
burned out from desert fighting.
Miss U.S.A.
puts quarters in the jukebox.

(Cue Black Sabbath's "War Pigs.")

As the bartender pours
frosted pitchers of cold ones
Haji steadies the pigskin
for kickoff,
Middle Eastern mascot
diverting destruction
of his homeland
with metaphorical mayhem
of misdirected
heroes.

*

Take Ten

After the last take
Haji opts out
of happy hour.
As the cast reproduces
their commercial
at the real bar,
Haji descends
the fated 12 steps
to the church basement.
While the chosen few
raise perfect mugs
of branded beer
as free advertisement,
Haji & his motley crew
raise empty hands,
sullying their names
as real alcoholics.

PRELUDE TO A POSTMODERN
PERSIAN PUPPET DANCE

Despite the visibility of strings
on descending angels,
Haji requires
theatrical suspension
of disbelief.

Rendered picaresque
by British Iran-o-phile J.J. Morier,
Haji found himself transformed
by Persian translator M.H. Isfahani,
re-appropriation of his origins
subtly rewriting
The Adventures of Hajji Baba of Isphan,

His figurative stage thus set,
Haji leaps from the book
and into folklore,
a postmodern dervish
song and dance man
strung out on letters
arranged to define him,
tracks of his failed journey
recorded on the stage.

IRAN AS SPECTACLE
(AN ORIENTALIST BURLESQUE)

Act I: The Persian Puppet Prepares his own Stage

On the tarmac at Mehrabad Airport
Haji leaves authentic experiences
of the old country behind him,
severing all strings
that root him to the land,
transplants images
on the plane's screen:
movies from *Argo* and *Aladdin*
to *Not Without My Daughter*,
300: Rise of an Empire.
Overnight from Paris
he completes *Shahs of Sunset*
as the sun rises
over NYC.

Hopping out of a cab
with the surface levity
of a Hollywood production,
Haji struts loose-limbed
down streets alone
singing his same old theme song
(*Haji Baba, Haji Baba!*),
a Persian Rhinestone Cowboy
on Broadway
working the grand narrative
of his foreign origins
into a new musical:

REVIEWS:

"Not since Ali Hakim, the Persian peddler in *Oklahoma!* has a minor Middle Eastern character lit up the grand stage."

—Ryan Seacrest, Executive Producer of *Shahs of Sunset*

"Heh heh heh. Heck of a show!"

—George W. Bush, Former American President

"O, O, O, that Rumi rag.
It's so erotic.
So exotic!"

—Azar Nafisi, author of *Reading Lolita in Tehran*

"With so much trouble in the region, it's great to let go and laugh at it all."

—Henry Kissinger, former Secretary of State

Act II

Against a backdrop of Persepolis
a line of bearded mullahs
covered in chadors
kick like Rockettes:

"There's no business like our faux business.
It's the only business we know.
Everything about it is revealing!
We humbly pray beneath gold ornate ceilings!"

These Muslim Ethel Mermans steal the show
(literally pick-pocketing pieces
of the Styrofoam set
spray-painted in silver and gold).

(Cue Britney Spears' "Oops I did it Again" juxtaposed with
Rimsky-Korsakov's "Scheherazade's Belly Dance before the
Sultan in Bra and Panties.")

A bevy of vulnerable pouty Persian beauties
in need of both saving and spanking,
led on leashes by mullahs
through a dark forest,
required chadors veiling
their hair
V-ing open
at vaginas.
(The artist Nicky Nodjoumi signs his name in red paint
along the lower right side of the stage.)

Act III

Stagehands lay down
Persian carpet
on top of brown-yellow shag,
haul in sectional sofa
and worn La-Z-Boy,
along with side table
holding rotary dial phone,
then wood-paneled
Magnavox
with meshy-macrame speaker
and clunky dial changer.

Scene I

Retro phone rings. Nameless 8-year-old Iranian-American boy answers.

Boy: Hello?

Anonymous caller in thick Texas accent: Hey boy, you go tell your
                 daddy to take you and your family back to *I-Ran*!

Boy: Excuse me? What do you mean?

Anonymous caller in thick Texas accent: You heard me, boy. We
                 want you *I-rain-ians* out of the neighborhood by
                 tomorrow... or we'll burn your house down!

                          Click!

Boy: Mom! Mom! There's a guy saying we have to move or
                 he's going to burn our house! Mom! (running off stage)

Scene II

Nightline with Ted Koppel plays on television. Recurring images of
American hostages, Ayatollah Khomeini's beard, Iranians burning
American flag, President Jimmy Carter saying a prayer, etc.

Boy sits playing Monopoly with best friend Benjamin Martinez in
front of TV. His Iranian father, clearly drunk in La-Z-Boy, pretends
to read *Wall Street Journal* upside down.

Retro phone rings. Keeps ringing. Boy answers.

Boy: *Hello? Salaam Amme Ezzat! Chetori? Bale. Babam injast.*
(to Father):   Dad, it's Aunt Ezzat. You better talk to her. She's
               crying hysterically.

Boy sits and rolls dice. Moves car onto Park Place. Pays his friend rent.

Father (instantly sober in fear): *Baradaram marde last???!!! Be qatal?*

Boy (whispering to friend): Holy shit. He's saying they killed my
                uncle…his brother.

Boy's friend: Jesus. Who?

Boy (pointing to Iranian flag burners on TV): Those guys.

Father hangs up phone. Reaches under La-Z-Boy for ½ full bottle
of vodka. Chugs it all in a few seconds. Falls forward onto Monopoly
Board. (Chants of "Down Down USA" on TV.)

Act IV

Mixing the high and the low
sacred and profane,
a riff on *ghazal* couplets
from the old Persian masters

Karabala mourners in black
beating bloody backs
in time to barefoot
dervish drummer boys

turning and turning
around belly dancing
burlesque babes
in black butterfly braziers
batting long lashes,
their charcoal outlined eyes
orgasmic oriental,
causing western men
in the audience
to erect tents
in the desert
of Middle Eastern
desire.

The producers go for broke:
oil wells rising
and falling center stage
in time to Mecca prayers,
one dancer's high heel
striking a new well,
spewing onto the audience

holding up hands
to keep from facing
the dirty business
of production,
one Macbeth Mother
rubbing her son's hands
with torn pages
from the playbill
and a bottle
of sanitizer.

Act V

Oh Haji, Haji,
wherefore art thou Haji?
Latent star of the show
ironically upstaged
by your own brand of mischief,
your go-to Orientalist themes played out
like your clichéd Persian style.
How quickly folks forget
their eponymous
hybrid hero.

But just as they yawn
and check their phones
a rumbling through the building
like 20 million NYC subways
shakes the crowd
from complacency!

The ceiling cracks.
A prophetic light
subsumes the stage
as if marking the spot
of an exclamation point
shooting like an arrow
down from the sky   !

                                    !

                    !

Faster than a racist judgment,
more powerful than
American hegemony
in the Middle East—
Look! Up in the air!
It's absurd! It's insane!
It's…our beloved Haji Baba
straight out of *Dr. Strangelove*,
riding on the back
of Major "King" Kong's
nuclear missile
(re-branded with Persian script),
headed toward our theatre
like a *deus ex machina*!

(Cue obliterating Ka-BOOM!
followed by infamous
mushroom cloud.)

HAJI'S CAMPAIGN TO SUPPORT THE
TROOPS BECOMES A REAL DRAG

At a bar outside Baghdad
lady-boy Haji wraps a silk scarf
(gift from a Marine named Steve)
around his Adam's apple,

croons karaoke Culture Club
with a missing button on his blouse,
making musky men gaze
through clouds of cigar smoke.

Downtown we'll drown
We're in our never splendor
Flowers showers
Who's got the new boy gender?

If only the soldiers' wives knew—
tying yellow ribbons around trees
back in Oklahoma—
how their husbands let him sit

hard on their laps, run his fingers
through their buzz cut hair,
whispering, "You packing heat
or are you just glad to see me?"

Of course he's burning out
from acting so hot
as they all cop a feel
to see if they're real;

he considers it a sacrifice,
his small supporting role
to keep their little G.I. Joes
standing at attention.

Wobbling over in high heels,
he catches himself in time
for the chorus: *I'll tumble for ya,
I'll tumble for ya, I'll tumble...*

HAJI'S RECIPE FOR
A TELEVISED DISASTER

Dusting healthy children with powdered sugar,
Haji hauls construction site rubble
in front of western reporters hungry
for scenes erotically catastrophic,
lays sexed-up druggie rich teens
wearing last night's club clothes
in a vat of spoiling tomatoes.

For authentic flavor barefoot Haji
approaches the news vans.
Watching them salivate
as make-up cakes their faces
(mic check testing 1, 2, 3),
he sells them salted ears
of charcoal-roasted corn.

HAJI'S SCARLET LETTER

Let Haji begin with an Arabic *alef*,
first order of creation,
body of the beloved, etc.

("What shall I do?" asks Hafez.
"My teacher gave me no other letter
to memorize!")

Quelle difference [!]
from that American adulteress
ably accommodating
all ambiguity.

Haji's signifying " \ "
sword of Ali,
self-divides
& conquers
Adam as Alpha
& Omega
avec unity
& unicity
of Allah.

THIS LITTLE HAJI

This little Haji went to market.
This little Haji stayed home.
This little Haji chewed kebob.
This little Haji gnawed bone.
This little Haji cried, "We little Hajis are all of us alone."

This little Haji pointed to that little Haji and said, "Same."
This little Haji asked that little Haji about the weather in exile.
I think we can see where this is going:
These little Hajis will seek connection for a while.
These little Hajis, for all their crying of "We,"
        are destined to remain single.

But agoraphobic Haji insists on going to the bazaar.
But hungry Haji attempts a Ramadan fast.
(I think we can see where this is going.)
But this little fading Haji thinks that he will last.
But this and that little Haji will end up in the past.

"Bam Bam!" into things crashed blind Haji
        who's always in search of the light.
"Chug Chug," drank drunk little Haji, stumbling
        toward the mosque to pray.
"Banal," says the reader who knew what was coming.
"Who cares?" roared hysterical Haji who called life
        a constant cliché.
"This little Haji!" cried this little Haji who never
        could get on his way.

HAJI DEFENDS HIS (T)RUTHFUL (T)ONE

And the well-known reviewer questioned
Haji's outdated didactic tone, arguing,
"In a postmodern age of relative truth,
how dare this poetaster proclaim universals?"

Over breakfast of bread and cheese
Haji cut a cross out of the paper,
took it to a seedy tattoo parlor
in downtown Newark,
the electric needle reproducing
painful pleasure
of his fundamental need
for acceptance
as the excerpted review bled
across his back,
permanent penance
for mockery-making
of transcendental signifier.

"(T)ake (t)hat you ra(t) bastard!"
said Haji, embodying his aesthetic principle
that eternally seeks to fuse spirit and letter.

And the aforementioned reviewer passing by the window,
upon seeing Haji lying face down on a table,
his blood approaching the ink from the essay,
sneered at the clichéd rhetorical stance,
rubbing salt in an open wound.

HAJI AS APPROPRIATOR
OF THE ISLAMIC REPUBLIC

1.
On anniversary of the great revolution,
Haji holds the Stars and Stripes
soaked in kerosene
without affect, watches his fingers
objectively, like foreign objects,
strike a match.

Amid tired cries of Death to America!
Haji feels himself fumble
for an old Sony tape recorder
embedded in his chest
and presses play,
addressing the masses
in monotone voice:

"Had Plato been successful
at banishing poets from the ideal Republic
the government itself would have assumed their position
(see histories of all nations, from Austria to Zimbabwe).

Revolutions counter systems of power
by appropriating the matrix.
Students of the American hostage-taking in 1979
have become professors
of what went wrong.

My fellow flag-burners have been bused in
from rural areas
to the center of Tehran,
paid cash for an hour
of rallying cries.

Extending examples to poetry,
a genre long ago crossed
into indifference,
my aesthetic master
strategically paid
$5 a head
with instructions to cheer
on command,
unconditionally supporting
the poet as toppling
the authoritarian regime.
They could just as well
burn books,
capturing the evil spirit
of this versifier."

2.
At the poetry reading,
bored out of his gourd
with his own poetry,
Haji takes off his shoes
to step more literally
across the stage;
first left to right, then right to left,
his bread and butter strut
of his American and Persian traditions.

At last he's broken through
the public's clichéd perception,
shattered the illusive wall
between audience and performer.

Unlike few traditional poets before him
schooled in form,
he can look at his readers
like they are his bitches,
spitting hard words
less like verse,
more like punk
at its inception
(before doctoral dissertations
written on punk
or a Cleveland museum
of rock 'n roll).

Having stood up
in previous poems
to ruthless rulers
gives him a little clout.

So what if the proverbial suit-wearing
snoots rolled their eyes?
Criticism is dead.
As if to make his point,
Haji polls the crowd,
asking who else could give a shit
about standards
in the 21st century?

If such support isn't enough to trump
any old school critic who remains in the room,
consider that more poets remain in Iranian prisons
than anywhere in the world.

Let this empty chair represent
the empty chair set aside
at readings by PEN
to represent each writer
without freedom:

Prisoner #412 from Turkey,
Prisoner #113 from Russia,
Prisoner #338 from Iran.

Proclaiming himself metaphorical martyr,
Haji jumps up on the chair,
saying, "Oh Captain! My Captain!"
Not so much like Robin Williams
in *Dead Poets Society*
as Robin Williams pretending
to play that character
in *Dead Poets Society*,
a Brechtian show-trial foregrounding
limits of performance.

The same goes for the shift in voice
as he channels Liam Neeson channeling
the Irish activist Michael Collins.

(Enter actors in the role of police who surround Haji.)

(Haji, in Irish accent:)

"Ah, here come our friends, the censorship police,
working on behalf of snooty academic critics
teamed up with the Islamic Republic of Iran,
a consortium of repressive regimes

from the 20th century really.
They can jail us. They can shoot us.
They can conscript us.
They can use our heads as cannon balls
to shoot across the Atlantic at America.
But…But…we have a weapon!
More powerful than anything
in the arsenal of that mockery
of what once was the Persian Empire.
And that weapon is our refusal…
Our refusal to bow down to any order but our own.
Any institution but our own!
Their hired goons might come for me

(hired goons approach Haji);

they would like to shut me up;
jail me with all the others in their disgusting Evin Prison.
Rape me with all the others.
Shoot me. Who knows?

But I'd like to send them a message.
If they manage against my will to shut me up
who'll take my place?

(Hired goons close in upon resisters around Haji.)

"I can't hear you! Who'll take my place?"

(Violent clash between goons and protestors.)

"I need to know…if something happens,
I need to know who will replace me?
Can they replace you?"

(Goons haul Haji away.)

WHEN LIKE FRANKENSTEIN'S MONSTER THEY INSTALL HUMAN EYES INTO THE WOODEN HEAD OF THE PERSIAN PUPPET POET...

Out of nowhere a pair of black butterflies
lands upon his eyes.
Instead of the postcard beauty of Isfahan
or the pistachio vendor on a busy street,
he sees visions of text,
highly patterned wordplay
in the poetry of Hafez.

ELEMENTAL TRANSLATION: WATER

99 names of one God.
99 translations from one source text.
Bashō's famous frog haiku
returned Haji to water,
trans-lingual life source—
the one element so essential
his predecessors skipped it
for flat words
dead on arrival,
even faux-enlightened Americans
wet behind the ears—

Robert Hass's

The old pond—
A frog jumps in
Sound of water

Ginsberg's *kerplunk*—

at best dissect
the once-living poem.

If Haji couldn't hear
the authentic splash
of the actual amphibian
he'd at least reduce
the falsely figural,
transcending translation
with a real frog
leaping off the page
of the original source text.

(Set up of microphone onto aquarium
made to look like old pond
next to jar containing frog...)

"Wow Haji, you did it,
like Jackson Pollock's dripping
his brush off the canvas,
you made nature
literal medium
in the realistic age,
inserting life
into death
of poetry troped
too far beyond origins."

In the beginning was physical semblance
of an ancient pond
and a live frog jumped in it
as if to prove
its very being,
giving shape
to primordial origins.

Those who have ears to hear,
let them here.

(Haji takes frog from jar,
holds him high above aquarium,
lets him jump...)

HAJI'S EKPHRASTIC MENTAL MAPPING

Loathing the clichéd striptease,
Haji lays bare
the mapping of his mind,
submitting brain scans
for audience approval,
his frontal white lobe
like negative space
of modernist abstractions
around micro-explosions
of synapses,
Pollock-esque splatters
of orange and red,
primordial topography
of all his desire,
pinball wizard
lighting up the screen
with such a supple wrist,
medium as message,
part and particle
of the machine.

When Haji showers in the locker room with the great Persian masters in a long tradition of verse, he can't help but look down to compare and despair, thus proving his own hypothesis that all art is born from suffering.

HAJI VS. ROSTAM

Provoked by the media,
Haji becomes as pugnacious as possible,
channeling that greatest of American poets,
Muhammad Ali, in front of the camera:

"Yeah, I'll fight Rostam and his dragon.
I'll float like a *parvane*, sting like a *zanbur*...
Come see the thrilla'
in ancient Persia.

I'm a bad man!"

If tired and tangled in the over 120,000 lines,
he'll play figurative trope-a-dope,
positioning the reader right where he wants him.

Rostam, trapped in the original *Shahnameh*
reproduces the same heroics with no deviation
beyond the way a conductor changes classical music.

Conversely, when Haji plays backgammon in Iran
he upsets the traditional masters
by rolling the dice a new way each time,
shaking and spitting them out of his mouth
and tossing them on the board with his feet.

If accused of lacking sufficient Persian authenticity,
there's hell to pay. From scratch, he'll chop up greens
for a quick batch of *qormeigh sabzi*
and refuse to share (an Iranian sin).

"I'm strong to the finish 'cause I eat my spinach.
I'm Haji Baba of Isfahan!
I'm so postmodern Iranian, the hair on my chest
takes the shape of Persian letters
from Hedayat's *The Blind Owl*."

If such a move weren't sufficient enough,
he steps into the shower with a razor,
erasing the story of erasure.

HAJI HAIKU

Worn tap shoes hanging
on power lines in Shiraz…
first stars at twilight.

The mullah's daughter…
Hadith forbidding tattoos
tattooed on her thigh.

Tampa, Florida…
mosque minaret ornaments
hung on X-mas trees.

PO BIZ

You gotta get a gimmick!
　　　　　　—Bette Midler, *Gypsy*

With doe-eyed
Natalie Wood
seductive gazes
at an audience hungry
for ethnic reduction
Haji summons a syringe
from offstage,
rolls up a sleeve
of his silk shirt
to draw first blood
from olive skin
ripe for the pricking.

Armed with fresh ink,
he paints humdrum
hegemonic towns
red with the shame
of his difference,
signing his name
like the last line
of a *ghazal* couplet,
conceptual Shia' martyr
figuratively dying
for his art.

HAJI'S WATERBOARDING

I've lost it all my life all lost—
the sky the earth the moon all lost.
Don't hand me wine. Pour it in my mouth.
(I've even lost the way to my mouth.)
　　　　　—Jalaluddin Rumi

At one with a pitcher of water,
he channels Rumi,
the Other pouring wine
down his gullet, a vessel
without agency,
"the hand"
sans possession—
like the French that killed
the spirit of the letter
along with the author—
waterboarding the bastard
who insists he's empty
of all meaning.

Inspector:　　So...*Monsieur* Haji, you are *z'ee* front for an
　　　　　　　American poet, no?

Haji:　　　　(No reply)

Inspector:　　Perhaps your throat is too dry to talk. Maybe you
　　　　　　　would like some of water. Perhaps you will drink it,
　　　　　　　how do *z'ey* say, in the American manner?

(One gloved hand pinches the nose, the other pours a pitcher of
water down the throat.)

Inspector:　　*Et comme ça,* we shorten the poetic line *z'at* your
　　　　　　　predecessor, *Monsieur* Olson, predicated on *z'ee*
　　　　　　　breath, no? (Haji gasps for air.)

Inspector: *Dites-moi, qui est Monsieur Sedarat?*

Haji: I do not know the man.

(Inspector relentlessly pours pitcher after pitcher of water down Haji's throat.)

Haji: "Okay okay!" (coughing) Please! No more! I did meet him once…before.

Inspector: Before what?

Haji: He died as romantic martyr…for poetry.

Inspector: So *Monsieur* Haji. We are finished for now. We arrive at your post-confession. I think at this point you…how do *z'ey* say, get the pitcher?

LUNAR POLITICS

When Haji photo-shops the moon,
replacing red-white-blue
of America
with red-green-white
of the Islamic Republic,
he's less politicizing the age-old satellite
than attempting to get an artistic rise
out of the 24-hour viewing public;
less stage-setting for the storming of embassies
than provoking outraged talking heads
by pretending one nation
under a hegemonic god
can own outer space.
Forbidden to depict Mohammad in image,
Haji scripts verse in metrically Arabic feet:

"The prophet was here."
                              Moon, 600 CE

HAJI'S RUBAIYYAT

Come, fill the cup, and in the fire of Spring
Your Winter-garment of repentance fling:
The bird of time has but a little way
To flutter—and the bird is on the wing.
— Omar Khayyam/Edward Fitzgerald

I could rationalize the stars, Khayyam,
Make much out of the man I think I am;
My quatrains still would produce empty rhymes,
A song to hear but not to understand.

The bowl of fire once used to hold the day
(Now a subject of anthropology)
Is filled with fissures. All substance escapes
From every broken word I try to say.

The bird may very well be on the wing,
But there is nothing left for him to sing;
His throat is dry and wine no longer wets
His whistle to sound his inner being.

Is it enough to inhabit silence?
Is it enough to sit in the dark since
It is impossible to prove myself?
I've done the math and found I make no sense.

This age still mourns the absent nightingale
And would revive its songs: traditional
Sounds of nature where spirit and matter
Make music that means something beautiful.

The bird beak's screech like nails on a chalk board,
The needle's scratch on a broken record,
Have overplayed the Persian romance themes
(Traces of which are seldom ever heard).

I should've been the song itself before
The Fall, when constructors of meaning bore
Their name by craft: "Attar" became "druggist";
"Assar," "oil presser"; "Khayyam," "tent maker."

Called "Haji," a name self-chosen, I've yet
To make my Mecca pilgrimage, I've yet
To make a thing of myself worth saying.
When asked, "What do you do?" I say, "I've yet."

Oh for the afterlife! Oh for the voice
Of Allah to tell me I have no choice
But to submit and save my hopeless soul;
I'd find myself with angels and rejoice.

But nothing is determined in this world.
My only fate is played out in the whirl
Of a dervish around an emptiness
That I inhabit but can never fill.

Take me as critic of your Rubaiyyat
Or else leave me as nothing, a whole note,
Blank oval in a song with no meaning
That sings of who I am by what I'm not.

AH GEE, HAJI

Geewilikers, shucks, gosh darn!
There's rumors you're more Midwest
than Middle East.

A mother born in Illinois
like Robert Fitzgerald,
humdinger of a translator
with affected British accent?
Back in his Harvard days
that poser didn't know
his Horace from his Dr. Seuss.

Admit it, Farmer Ted,
aren't you sometimes
 a little more at home
in predictable flatlands
of corn fields?
Wouldn't you just as much order
coleslaw as *torshi*?

Doesn't Berryman's thwarting
of mainstream America,
Pound's potato farms in Idaho
ultimately mean as much
as Yosij or Shamlu
"radically" breaking the rhyme?

Transplanting yourself in NYC
just relocated fo transgressions
at the Port Authority bus station,
left you standing on a street corner
fresh off a Greyhound

like Lou Reed's Sweet Jane,
a suitcase in your hand
full of broken rules of verse
to make critics roll their eyes.

In his fantasy the crowd at the show begged his curtain not to close. Haji reassured them, saying, "Though I must go the way of all flesh, my childishly obsessive grandiose spirit will remain."

"But how?" Haji imagined one of his fantasy fans asking.

And Haji replied, "Just because you've gotten the monkey off your back, doesn't mean the circus has left town."

RETURN TO THE CIRCUS ANIMALS

Among Americans he deemed "the greats,"
The best wrote over forms. He tried with Yeats,

But it just sounded like mere parody
Opposed to Dickinson's slight mimicry

Of hymns, or Eliot with Donne's mermaids,
Perhaps Thoreau's revised jeremiads.

He sought such style and sought for it in vain,
His post-poetic age quoting Lil' Wayne

And warning labels printed on paint cans.
America's verse sold out, but Iran's

Conservative, despite dropping the rhyme.
He'd locate a new postmodernism

Within a sort of Bhabhaian "third space"
Hybrid identity. He once erased

The second line of Persian ghazals where
Beloveds lived. (The form just disappeared.)

But that's no more than "Reading Lolita..."
Just like his mistranslated *qasidas*,

Too clever with the monorhyme: sing song
With little depth. Indeed he did belong

To surface-level western depictions,
Hence "Haji," his persona creation

Who walked out of a picaresque novel
Set in Iran, a stereotypical

Performer of a Persian hypocrite
Full of the same appropriative shit.

He sought to mine "the bone shop of the heart"
But couldn't make his own decadent art.

A record of his struggle to be new
Proved ultimately the best he could do.

ABOUT THE AUTHOR

Roger Sedarat is an Iranian-American poet and translator. He is the author of three previous poetry collections: *Dear Regime: Letters to the Islamic Republic*, which won Ohio UP's 2007 Hollis Summers' Prize, *Ghazal Games* (Ohio UP, 2011), and *Foot Faults: Tennis Poems* (David Robert Books, 2016). A recent recipient of the Willis Barnstone Translation Prize, he teaches poetry and literary translation in the MFA Program at Queens College, City University of New York.

ABOUT THE ARTIST

Nicky Nodjoumi is an Iranian artist known for his political themes. He earned his Bachelor's degree at the Tehran University of Fine Arts and his MFA from The City College of New York. His paintings are included in the collections of the Metropolitan Museum of Art in New York, the British Museum in London, Guggenheim Museum in Abu Dhabi, the DePaul Art Museum in Chicago, and the National Museum of Cuba. In 2014, Nodjoumi had a solo exhibition at the Cleveland Institute of Art titled *The Accident*. He lives and works in Brooklyn.

THE TENTH GATE PRIZE

Jennifer Barber, *Works on Paper*, 2015
Roger Sedarat, *Haji as Puppet*, 2016
Lisa Sewell, *Impossible Object*, 2014

INTERNATIONAL EDITIONS

Kajal Ahmad (Alana Marie Levinson-LaBrosse, Mewan Nahro
    Said Sofi, and Darya Abdul-Karim Ali Najin, trans., with
    Barbara Goldberg), *Handful of Salt*
Keyne Cheshire (trans.), *Murder at Jagged Rock: A Tragedy by
    Sophocles*
Jean Cocteau (Mary-Sherman Willis, trans.), *Grace Notes*
Yoko Danno & James C. Hopkins, *The Blue Door*
Moshe Dor, Barbara Goldberg, Giora Leshem, eds.,
    The Stones Remember: Native Israeli Poets
Moshe Dor (Barbara Goldberg, trans.), *Scorched by the Sun*
Lee Sang (Myong-Hee Kim, trans.), *Crow's Eye View: The Infamy
    of Lee Sang, Korean Poet*
Vladimir Levchev (Henry Taylor, trans.), *Black Book of the
    Endangered Species*

THE WASHINGTON PRIZE

Nathalie F. Anderson, *Following Fred Astaire*, 1998
Michael Atkinson, *One Hundred Children Waiting for a Train*, 2001
Molly Bashaw, *The Whole Field Still Moving Inside It*, 2013
Carrie Bennett, *biography of water*, 2004
Peter Blair, *Last Heat*, 1999
John Bradley, *Love-in-Idleness: The Poetry of Roberto Zingarello*,
    1995, 2nd edition 2014
Christopher Bursk, *The Way Water Rubs Stone*, 1988
Richard Carr, *Ace*, 2008
Jamison Crabtree, *Rel[AM]ent*, 2014
Jessica Cuello, *Hunt*, 2016
B. K. Fischer, *St. Rage's Vault*, 2012
Linda Lee Harper, *Toward Desire*, 1995
Ann Rae Jonas, *A Diamond Is Hard But Not Tough*, 1997
Frannie Lindsay, *Mayweed*, 2009
Richard Lyons, *Fleur Carnivore*, 2005
Elaine Magarrell, *Blameless Lives*, 1991
Fred Marchant, *Tipping Point*, 1993, 2nd edition 2013
Ron Mohring, *Survivable World*, 2003
Barbara Moore, *Farewell to the Body*, 1990
Brad Richard, *Motion Studies*, 2010
Jay Rogoff, *The Cutoff*, 1994
Prartho Sereno, *Call from Paris*, 2007, 2nd edition 2013
Enid Shomer, *Stalking the Florida Panther*, 1987
John Surowiecki, *The Hat City After Men Stopped Wearing Hats*, 2006
Miles Waggener, *Phoenix Suites*, 2002
Charlotte Warren, *Gandhi's Lap*, 2000
Mike White, *How to Make a Bird with Two Hands*, 2011
Nancy White, *Sun, Moon, Salt*, 1992, 2nd edition 2010
George Young, *Spinoza's Mouse*, 1996

THE HILARY THAM CAPITAL COLLECTION

Nathalie Anderson, *Stain*

Mel Belin, *Flesh That Was Chrysalis*

Carrie Bennett, *The Land Is a Painted Thing*

Doris Brody, *Judging the Distance*

Sarah Browning, *Whiskey in the Garden of Eden*

Grace Cavalieri, *Pinecrest Rest Haven*

Cheryl Clarke, *By My Precise Haircut*

Christopher Conlon, *Gilbert and Garbo in Love*
    & *Mary Falls: Requiem for Mrs. Surratt*

Donna Denizé, *Broken like Job*

W. Perry Epes, *Nothing Happened*

David Eye, *Seed*

Bernadette Geyer, *The Scabbard of Her Throat*

Barbara G. S. Hagerty, *Twinzilla*

James Hopkins, *Eight Pale Women*

Brandon Johnson, *Love's Skin*

Marilyn McCabe, *Perpetual Motion*

Judith McCombs, *The Habit of Fire*

James McEwen, *Snake Country*

Miles David Moore, *The Bears of Paris*
    & *Rollercoaster*

Kathi Morrison-Taylor, *By the Nest*

Tera Vale Ragan, *Reading the Ground*

Michael Shaffner, *The Good Opinion of Squirrels*

Maria Terrone, *The Bodies We Were Loaned*

Hilary Tham, *Bad Names for Women*
    & *Counting*

Barbara Louise Ungar, *Charlotte Brontë, You Ruined My Life*
    & *Immortal Medusa*

Jonathan Vaile, *Blue Cowboy*

Rosemary Winslow, *Green Bodies*

Michele Wolf, *Immersion*

Joe Zealberg, *Covalence*

OTHER WORD WORKS BOOKS

Annik Adey-Babinski, *Okay Cool No Smoking Love Pony*
Karren L. Alenier, *Wandering on the Outside*
Karren L. Alenier, ed., *Whose Woods These Are*
Christopher Bursk, ed., *Cool Fire*
Barbara Goldberg, *Berta Broadfoot and Pepin the Short*
Frannie Lindsay, *If Mercy*
Elaine Magarrell, *The Madness of Chefs*
Marilyn McCabe, *Glass Factory*
Ann Pelletier, *Letter That Never*
Ayaz Pirani, *Happy You Are Here*
W. T. Pfefferle, *My Coolest Shirt*
Jacklyn Potter, Dwaine Rieves, Gary Stein, eds.,
Cabin Fever: Poets at Joaquin Miller's Cabin
Robert Sargent, *Aspects of a Southern Story*
     & *A Woman from Memphis*
Fritz Ward, *Tsunami Diorama*
Amber West, *Hen & God*
Nancy White, ed., *Word for Word*

CPSIA information can be obtained
at www.ICGtesting.com
Printed in the USA
FSOW01n1400230217
31140FS